SPORTS TO THE EXTREME

EXTREME BIKING

Jeanne Nagle

rosen publishing's
rosen central

NEW YORK

Published in 2016 by The Rosen Publishing Group, Inc.

29 East 21st Street, New York, NY 10010

Library of Congress Cataloging-in-Publication Data

Nagle, Jeanne.
Extreme biking/Jeanne Nagle.—First Edition.
    pages cm.—((Sports to the Extreme))
Includes bibliographical references and index.
Audience: Grades: 5–8.
ISBN 978-1-4994-3565-8 (Library bound) — ISBN 978-1-4994-3567-2 (Paperback) —
ISBN 978-1-4994-3568-9 (6-pack)
1. Bicycle motocross—Juvenile literature. I. Title.
GV1049.3.N35 2015
796.6'22—dc23

2014047699

Manufactured in the United States of America

CONTENTS

INTRODUCTION

Riding a bike is terrific exercise. Coasting through a park on a summer day can be very relaxing. In some parts of the world, bicycles take the place of cars as a major form of transportation. But as fans of extreme sports know, biking can also be a heart-thumping, lump-in-the-throat adventure. And they wouldn't have it any other way.

Extreme biking is designed for those who would rather see a blur flash all around them than casually take in the scenery. In addition to speed, this sport is a test of dexterity, balance, and control. Freestyle riders need to combine all these factors with an active imagination because they must come up with tricks that are difficult to pull off and interesting to watch. Yet no matter how skilled or prepared they are, extreme bike riders are constantly aware that the terrain they travel is unpredictable and can bring disaster at any moment.

Biking to the extreme comes in two basic forms. Mountain biking is aptly named, because cliffs, peaks, and impressive hills are where most of the action in this type of riding takes place. Mountains are not involved in bicycle motocross, better known by its abbreviation, BMX. Yet there are plenty of dirt hills on a BMX racing track, as well as other obstacles challenging riders at every turn. Additionally, there

4

Two mountain bikers fly down a specially designed course. Steep declines, tree roots, stones, and other obstacles are part of the challenge and fun of extreme biking.

are several competitive styles under each category as well, breaking down the sport even further.

Let's face it. Some people are perfectly happy riding bikes for fun or as a way to get from one place to another. Others enjoy getting their thrills secondhand by watching riders hurl themselves down mountains or take their machines airborne while breaking from the pack on a dirt track. For those who are interested in taking calculated chances, pushing themselves and their specially outfitted bicycles to the edge and back, extreme biking is the sport of their dreams.

CHAPTER ONE

PEDALING THROUGH HISTORY

Kirkpatrick Bicycle, 1839.

Phantom Bicycle, 1869.

Bicyclette, 1879.

Kangaroo Bicycle, 1884.

Otto Dicycle, 1881.

"Rudge," 1884.

Examples of bicycles from the nineteenth century. The Kirkpatrick (*upper left*), the first pedal bike, is named for blacksmith and inventor Kirkpatrick Macmillan.

The history of bicycles dates back to the 1800s, when a number of two-wheeled, self-propelled machines were invented. Bikes as they are known today can be traced back to a vehicle created by a blacksmith in Scotland. This vehicle used a rod connected to the pedals to create forward motion. The invention closest to the modern bicycle, though, was the veloc-ipede, first built in Paris in the 1860s. Riding these bicycles became popular in Britain and America shortly after they were introduced in France.

Extreme biking is another matter, though. Chances are

there have been riders who have ridden in a challenging, even daredevil manner on their own practically since bicycling began. But that is not the same thing as the origins of this extreme sport. For that, one needs to move ahead about a century from when the first bikes were built, to 1970s California, to see how both mountain biking and BMX got their starts.

KLUNKERS VS. MOUNT TAM

The town of Fairfax, California, rests near the foot of a mountain that, at its highest peak, stands more than 2,500 feet (785 m) high. Its name is Mount Tamalpais, but it is more commonly known simply as Mount Tam. It was on the rocky trails of Mount Tam that extreme mountain biking was officially born.

The mountain-biking movement was led by a small group of cycling fans in their twenties. Among them was Joe Breeze, who is considered to be the "godfather of mountain biking." Breeze bought a beat-up 1940s Schwinn bicycle with balloon tires, which were wider and tougher than road-bike tires, and a strong frame. The machine was called a paper-boy bike because paper delivery boys were the most common riders of the model in the 1930s and '40s. In biking circles, the old Schwinn was referred to as a "klunker."

After stripping the bike down to the bare bones so that it would be lighter to carry up hills, Breeze took it up to the summit, or top, of Mount Tam and launched it and himself down an old dirt road once used by a railway company. After that, riding at breakneck speed down Mount Tam on fixed-up klunkers became a regular thing with Breeze and his friends. Gary Fisher, Charlie Kelly, Otis Guy, Tom Richey, Wende Cragg, Breeze, and others would compete to see who could reach the bottom of the road in the fastest time. Joe Breeze won many of those early races.

GREASING THE SKIDS

Klunkers were able to to take the punishment of racing off-road and downhill better than road bikes, but they weren't by any means perfectly suited to the task. The brakes of these adapted bikes were often overworked on flying downhill runs, burning off the grease that kept them working in the process. Before they could take another trip down Mount Tam, racers would need to replace or "repack" the grease on their brakes, which had burned up on one trip down the mountain. That is why the first competition to take place on the mountain became known as the Repack race.

As word got out about what Joe Breeze and his friends were doing, other extreme-biker wannabes in the area began showing up and entering races. Twenty-two Repacks were run between 1976 and 1979. Riders and the event organizers were busy with jobs and road races. There were two reunion Repacks held, one in 1983 and one in 1984.

MOUNTAIN BIKING BECOMES A BREEZE

Trained in architecture, engineering, and metalworking, Breeze had experience building specialized road bikes for his own use and for other cyclists to race. While the modified klunkers they had been using served their purpose well, mountain bikers felt that they would be better off riding a bike designed especially for rough riding. Breeze answered the call for a true mountain bike by building the Breezer in 1977. Nine more of this model were built over the course of a year. The frames of the bikes were made of aircraft-quality steel tubing, while the handlebars and brakes were repurposed motorcycle parts.

Several mountain bikes from the original batch of ten created by Joe Breeze in 1977–78 have been displayed in museums across the United States and around the world. Among them is Breezer No. 1, the very first mountain bike Breeze built from scratch. For twenty-five years, visitors to the Oakland Museum could see it as part of an exhibit on this history of California. In 2011, after making a brief stop—one day—at the Mountain Bike Hall of Fame, Breezer No. 1 found its way to the Smithsonian Institution in Washington, D.C.

The second Breezer, which was built for Breeze's friend and fellow mountain bike pioneer Charlie Kelly, is in the Mountain Bike Hall of Fame. A third Breezer has found a home in Osaka, Japan, in a cycling museum supported by Shimano, a sports and leisure company known for manufacturing outstanding bike parts.

Joe Breeze, poses in 2004 in Berlin behind the wheel of a folding bike he built. Breeze is credited with "inventing" the mountain bike and popularizing the sport.

OFFICIALLY OFF-ROAD

The Repack races down Mount Tam were just the start of mountain biking's road to becoming a popular extreme sport. Local television news stations picked up on the story of the young men and women who were taking wild rides down mountain roads. Kids and young adults who lived in the area scrambled up Mount Tam with their own bikes to take part in Repacks. Attention from outside California soon followed.

Although the Repack races themselves did not last much beyond 1979, their influence on competitions in the sport is amazing. During the early 1980s, amateur mountain biking competitions that were a lot like the Repack sprang up across California. In 1983, the National Off-Road Bicycle Association (NORBA) was founded to organize the sport. With a governing body in place, mountain bike races went from being informal gatherings that gave riders bragging rights to official events where they could win titles and even a bit of prize money.

DOWN IN THE DIRT

Even though it was a documentary about motorcycle racing, the 1971 film *On Any Sunday* began with a shot of kids speeding around a hilly dirt track in California. The bike riders were imitating motorcycle racers as they pedaled furiously, popped into jumps, and cut into curves and sharp turns. In that short opening scene, moviegoers were witnessing the extreme sport that would soon become BMX racing.

No doubt kids had been riding off-road, in the dirt, long before the film hit theaters. They probably had also been staging casual races on dirt tracks created by the repeated pounding of their bike tires across an empty lot or field. But in the 1970s, the sport of BMX began to take shape. What started in Southern California spread across the country. Hundreds of riders in many different cities began adapting their bicycles for off-road use—the preferred bike for such fix-ups was the Schwinn Stingray—and performing tricks as they raced to reach the finish line.

WHERE THE BUFFALO SOLDIERS ROAMED

A corps of black soldiers in the United States Army during the 1890s might very well be one of the oldest groups of off-road bikers ever. Buffalo Soldiers, as American soldiers of color after the Civil War were known, of the 25th Infantry Regiment took part in an experiment. They wanted to see if bicycle travel might be better for the military than marching or riding horses. Their bikes were designed to travel over land that had no roads and few, if any, trails or paths. Food, cooking materials, a tent, and other equipment, as well as spare parts and tires, made the already heavy steel bicycles even heavier.

Among the successes of the unit was a trip from Fort Missoula in Montana to Yellowstone National Park in Wyoming. A difficult ride from the fort to St. Louis, Missouri—totaling 1,900 miles (approximately 3,058 km)—would turn out to be their last. The bicycle corps stopped under orders, thanks to increased conflict with Spain, then faded away.

A TALE OF TWO BIKING SPORTS

BMX racing began as an imitation of motocross, a sport started in the 1920s where motorcyclists ride several laps around a rough dirt course. It's hard to say if motocross riders were flattered, but they did take an active interest in the new bicycling sport.

One of the first motorcycle racers to get involved in BMX was Scot Breithaupt. A motocross champion, Breithaupt built himself a practice course, complete with mud pit and built-in jumps, on an empty lot in Long Beach, California. In November 1970 he invited kids, many of whom had been watching him and copying his moves, to race their bicycles on his track. There were beginner, novice, and expert races, and the winners in each division were given a trophy from Breithaupt's personal motocross collection. These weekly races became so popular that

Female riders on the track during the 1925 International Six Days Trial off-road motorcycle race. Events such as these were the inspiration for BMX races.

Breithaupt built more courses around Southern California. To keep all the action organized, he formed the statewide organization Bicycle United Motocross Society, or BUMS.

Other people from motocross who influenced BMX racing include Ernie Alexander and George Esser. A motocross promoter in California, Alexander founded the first national BMX governing body, the National Bicycle Association, in 1973. Later, the organization was renamed the National Bicycle Motocross Association, to make its connection to BMX clearer. While running the National Motorcycle League (NML) in Florida, Esser opened NML tracks to BMX riders, and he cofounded the International Bicycle Motocross Federation (IBMXF) in 1981. Together with the American Bicycle Association, formed in 1977 in Arizona, these organizations led BMX racing into a bright and promising future.

CHAPTER TWO

EXTREMELY MODERN BIKING

Extreme biking has come a long way in its relatively short life as an organized sport. The number of participants for both mountain biking and BMX has swelled since the 1970s. According to a recent Outdoor Industry Foundation report, biking, including mountain biking and BMX, was the second-most-practiced outdoor activity reported by people of all ages. Events have sprung up all over the place to make room for those who want to compete. In addition to national and world championships, extreme biking is now also featured in the X Games and even the Olympics.

STYLE MATTERS

Both types of extreme biking have one certain style that seems to define them in the minds of spectators and riders alike. For mountain biking, that style is downhill. After all, it was the original mountain biking event, created by adventure seekers living near Mount Tam. Similarly, the first BMXers were known

BMX racers jockey for position at the 2011 Pan American Games in Guadalajara, Mexico. The roots of BMX racing are deep in the dirt.

for racing on a dirt track. Therefore, racing, in particular dirt racing, is forever linked first and foremost with BMX.

However, each of these forms of extreme biking also has other styles associated with it. Riders can pick and choose which style best suits their strengths as a rider. They may choose to specialize, or they may choose to build their skills and enter competitions in all the different styles. Anyone who wants to experience the thrill of extreme biking should first think about the full menu of options that the sport has to offer.

MOUNTAIN DO

Mountain biking started out as a sport where, as the name clearly states, bikes were ridden down mountains. That is still the case today with downhill mountain biking, as well as enduro events. Cross-country riders also face hilly terrain, although the declines are not as steep as a mountain downhill trail. Off the mountain, there is still plenty of mountain-biking action during trials events.

DOWNHILL

Downhill races are typically the first style many people think of when they hear the

Strength and control vie with speed when mountain bikers are on the move. Dealing with challenging conditions is part of what makes this sport extreme.

words "mountain biking." Even though downhill riders may perform stunts, such as jumps and slides, during races to help them get to the finish line faster, basically they are all about speed going down a mountain.

Downhill tests riders' strength as well as their speed. Downhill racers have to keep control of a bike while rushing over lumps, bumps, stones, tree roots, and holes at speeds upward of 40 miles (about 64 km) an hour. Tremendous arm and leg strength are required to steer and keep the bike balanced and upright.

DESIGNED BY MOTHER NATURE

Downhill riders are, of course, competing against other people. In a lot of ways, though, downhill racing is also very much a case of rider against nature. Professional downhill courses are designed, meaning event organizers mark off a suitable path or trail down a lengthy incline. Certain elements, such as jumps and drops, may be added or improved. But when it comes down to it, most of the elements found on a downhill course are nature-made, not man-made.

CROSS-COUNTRY

In addition to flying down steep hillsides, mountain bikers test their endurance in cross-country, or distance, events. Riders complete the total mileage by riding several laps of a looped, marked course. Technical elements, such as descents and climbs, greet riders on each lap. Cross-country courses, which tend to be a mixed bag of different kinds of terrain, are definitely challenging, but they are not considered as difficult as downhill paths.

Distances covered by these races vary by age and level of experience of the rider. Younger riders might use the same course as older, more experienced riders, but they will do fewer laps around the course. The specifics of the race also determine the length and distance of cross-country races as well. For instance, cross-country eliminator races—where four riders compete in heats, or rounds, and the four fastest from each round compete for the title—are shorter than regular cross-country events. Likewise, cross-country marathon races are longer.

TRIALS AND ENDURO

Showing off their ability to keep their balance while completing several slick maneuvers is what draws riders to trials events. Traveling over a course or courses one section at a time, riders are required to take their bikes through and over a number of obstacles without putting their foot down to steady themselves. Obstacles can be both natural, such as rocks and logs, or man-made, including ramps, boxes, and stairs. Riders are allowed a specific amount of time to get through each section—there can be up to ten sections per event—and each section is completed at least twice by each rider. Judges watch the riders at each section carefully to see how they handle themselves and their bikes.

Trials events were first held in Europe in the 1980s. While still more popular in Europe than anywhere else, trials have also made a splash in the United States and Canada.

Another type of mountain bike event that started around the same time and is popular in Europe is known as enduro. These races are held in stages, on several different trails across one location. As with downhill, racers try to finish each stage as quickly as possible. They must go back up hills to get to each stage's start point, but the time it takes to get to each start is not counted against the rider, only the ride down.

BMX—OF COURSE

BMX riding takes its style cues from the nature of the courses on which events are run. Dirt racing forms arguably the biggest and most popular community of bicycle motocross racers. Yet anyone who has ever watched the X Games knows that vert (short for vertical) BMX is a high-octane, competitive version of the sport as well. Unlike vert riders, who perform within the curved parameters of a man-made obstacle, flatland riders excel on smooth, even, and—of course, as the name indicates—flat surfaces to pull out their best moves and tricks.

PULLING A STUNT

Basically, trials are a form of stunt riding. One basic trials stunt is called a track stand, which is being able to stand on the pedals of the bike without moving or falling over. It's easy to imagine what another move, the j-hop, looks like given its other name—a bunny hop. The front tire goes up first, followed by the back tire going up off the ground. The landing is done in the same order, with the front tire coming down first.

The skill known as ratcheting has riders pedaling ahead to keep moving forward but then pedaling backward to the start position. By completing only sections of a full-circle pedal at a time, trials riders can better move over stretches of bumpy terrain and through water without tipping and losing their balance.

A manual is another common stunt that is useful to trials riders. This involves pulling the front tire of the bike up off the ground—also known as popping a wheelie—and riding only on the back tire. When performing a manual, the rider does not do any pedaling, but instead moves forward due to the spinning of the back tire only. Pedaling while performing this maneuver makes it a totally different stunt, called a catwalk.

DIRT

Racing on dirt tracks is the traditional style of bicycle motocross. Up to eight competitors line up in a starting gate and are released out onto a twisty trail of dirt. Man-made hills give riders air, and berms—corners that are built up to rise into a curve—help them fight for position.

Dirt races can be run either as qualifiers, where winners of separate heats advance to the final race for the title, or for points. In the second case, every competitor races three times around a track, earning points for how well he or she rides and finishes.

Riders are assigned to a certain level of racing based on their age, gender, and experience level. Beginners are called novices.

A BMX racer climbs up a berm as she takes a curve, going full-tilt. Dirt BMX tracks are built in such a way to help and challenge riders.

The middle level is intermediate, and the highest level is expert. Bikes with 20-inch (about 51-centimeter) wheels, called class bikes, are the norm and are ridden by boys and girls at every experience level. Riders with cruise bikes, which have twenty-four-inch (around sixty-one-centimeter) tires, are divided by age and gender, but not by experience level.

VERT

Extreme bike riders often speak in a language all their own, especially when they are gathered together at a competition. For instance, BMX riders use the term "vert" to describe riding the length of a man-made course called a half-pipe. The word is also short for "vertical," meaning straight up and down—which is the position these bikers are in for just about their entire ride.

Of course, while simply racing up and down a curved wall on a bike is impressive itself, vert riders do so much more in competition. Getting air and performing tricks are important parts of this style of BMX as well. Air is another way of saying that riders soar to great heights with their bikes fully off the ground. Tricks include spins, grabs, and flips. Taking one or both feet off of the bike's pedals, or flinging a leg over the handlebars, in midair—and having everything back in place by the time the tires hit ground—are also crowd-pleasing moves during vert competitions.

STREET

Like vert, street BMX also takes place on a man-made course. Instead of a single half-pipe, however, riders wheel around on concrete or pavement trying to conquer many different obstacles. Anything from stairs and curbs to railings (called simply rails) and

A BMX biker gets some air beneath his tires as he makes use of the city pavement and even a brick wall during a ride.

cement barriers can be considered an obstacle on a street course. If riders can roll, jump, or spin over and around it, it's an obstacle.

Also known as "urban," because it usually takes place in a city environment, a pure form of this style of BMX is practiced by amateurs actually in the streets. Professionals in competition ride in specially designed parks. That is why street is also referred to as park BMX.

FLATLAND

Flatland is all about tricks without the boost that comes from jumps or the half-pipe. The location for this style of BMX is just where the name says—a large, flat area of land. Each rider's series of tricks, which have colorful names such as tailwhips and cyclones, are run together in a routine. Some people have compared riding flatland to dancing on a bike.

In the world of BMX, flatland has had its ups and downs. Years ago, this style was popular at events where different kinds of riding occurred. As other styles such as street became more popular, flatland temporarily took a backseat at all but a few BMX-related events. Then, in 2012, flatland was added to one of the biggest tours, sponsored by Mountain Dew. After that, it found its way back into the spotlight again.

CHAPTER THREE

BIKING INTO HIGH GEAR

Extreme biking is a fun and exciting sport that people of all ages and skill levels can enjoy. Of course, neither mountain biking nor BMX is necessarily a cheap activity. For those who simply want to practice extreme biking on their own without entering competitions, the costs can be reasonable. But anyone hoping to earn a title or a trophy should expect to lay out some serious cash, at least at first. Riders must have a solid, dependable bike designed for their style(s) of riding. Proper clothing, including safety gear, is also highly recommended.

WHAT A RIDE!

Gone are the days when bicyclists were forced to modify street bikes or fix up klunkers to experience a decent extreme ride. Now there are a number of companies that sell machines built specifically for mountain biking and BMX. While each manufacturer offers its own special spin on these types of bikes, the basics are the same: a frame, gears, two wheels, tires, pedals, and a seat.

HARD BODIES

The frame, meaning the body, of an off-road bike is built of stronger and heavier materials than a regular street bike. Mountain bikes and, especially, BMX bikes are pretty compact, which simply means they are smaller and their various parts are usefully closer together.

Handlebars, which control steering and also help determine how a rider is positioned on a bike, can be straight or rise up a bit on either end, with a slight dip in the middle over the wheel. The latter type are called riser handlebars. In general, mountain bike handlebars are more likely to be straight and flat. BMX handlebars have more of a rise to them, as a rule of thumb.

THE WHEEL THING

Like mountain bike and BMX frames, the wheels of off-road bikes are tough and designed to take a serious beating without

GET IT IN GEAR

Gears are what control the speed of a bike. Different gears make the wheels complete more or fewer rotations each time the rider pedals. The more rotations, or full spins, of the wheels, the faster the bike goes. Mountain bikes can have as many twenty-seven gears, while BMX bikes are strictly one-gear machines. In other words, BMX bikes depend a lot on a rider's pedal power.

bending or breaking. Wheels are made up of metal rims covered by rubber tires. Bike tires are sized by the radius or diameter, meaning the distance between edges of a circle after passing through the center. Tires for mountain bikes are either 26 or 29 inches (about 66 or 74 cm) in diameter, while BMX tires are a bit smaller at 20 inches (roughly 51 cm). Width is also important to a bicycle's tire size. Off-road bikes have tires that are bigger and wider than those on regular road or street bikes.

Another consideration is the tire's tread, which describes the ridged or grooved surface of the tire that touches the ground. On off-road bikes, the tread is typically thick and knobby. This design helps gain traction, which is a scientific way of saying that the tires are better able to make contact with the ground and push off from it so that more power is created to move the bike.

Mountain bike and BMX tires are designed to give riders more power and greater speed. The secret lies in the bumps and grooves of the tire tread.

SNOWY PEAKS, SANDY BOTTOMS

Off-road bicyclists are used to riding on dirt, mud, grass, and rocks. Snow is another matter altogether. To let riders in North America ride year-round, some bicycle manufacturers have created super-sized machines known as fat bikes. The frame and other parts of a fat bike are built to make room for large, bulky tires that, because of their width and low air pressure, help the machines travel over snow and sand.

In the snow, certain weather conditions make for a better fat-bike ride than others. There should not be too much snow, though, because the bike will get stuck in drifts. But too little snow, such as the slushy covering that would be on trails after temperatures rise and melting has begun, isn't good either. More important, fat bikes were meant for trail riding—not so much for fast, steep downhill runs.

SADDLE UP (OR DOWN)

Off-road bike seats, also known as saddles, are designed mainly to make things easy for riders. They are long and narrow up front and through the middle, to give the rider's legs room to pedal and move freely. An off-road saddle's back end, however, is fuller and

The shape of off-road bicycle saddles lets riders pump their pedals with greater ease. The front is thinner, so their legs don't rub or knock against the seat.

well-padded to be more comfortable and protective of a rider's "back end."

Perhaps more important than a mountain bike or BMX saddle's shape is its height when attached to the frame. Saddles should be carefully adjusted up or down depending on how long the rider's legs are. While seated, the rider should have a slightly bent leg with his or her foot on one pedal—not stretched straight or with the knee too close to the chest.

UNIFORMS, OF SORTS

Technically, off-road bikers could go out on their own and ride down a hill or race around a track in their street clothes. But that wouldn't be very smart (and event organizers would be pretty unhappy about it also). In order to be the most comfortable and to have the greatest range and ease of motion, extreme bikers wear various articles of clothing that make the most sense for their style of riding.

Extreme bike riders wear shirts called jerseys. Biking jerseys look a lot like regular shirts or light jackets, but they are designed specifically for bicyclists. The fabrics they are made of keep riders cool and dry by soaking up sweat. The shoulders have enough room in them so that

Bicycle jerseys are roomy and draw sweat from riders' bodies. Many are as stylish as they are comfortable and practical.

grasping the handlebars and steering are smooth moves. Little extras such as pockets and zippers are often added to cycling jerseys.

Early BMX racers imitated not only how motorcyclists raced around a dirt track but also what bikers wear. Motorcycle riders have been known to wear a lot of leather. Besides looking cool, leather clothing protects motorcyclists—from the weather and, more important, from getting too banged up in an accident. Leather is very strong, and it is less likely to shred or fall apart if a rider hits the ground at a high rate of speed. The full-length pants worn by many BMX riders are called leathers, in honor of traditional motorcycle clothing. The funny thing is that these days BMX pants are not actually made of leather but instead are most often nylon.

Mountain bikers usually favor clothes that help them cut through the air without resistance, meaning push-back caused by their motion. Their jerseys and pants fit very close, almost like a second skin.

HEAD-TO-TOE SAFETY

Mountain biking and BMX racing have a high level of danger associated with them. That is why those who participate in organized competitive events must be dressed in full-on safety gear or they won't even get up to the start line.

First and foremost in a serious biker's safety lineup should be a helmet. Some helmets also have a face guard attached for more protection, especially where the mouth and teeth are concerned.

The risk of wiping out or crashing is part of the excitement of extreme biking. However, riders should do all they can to minimize the danger.

Protecting one's eyes from dust, flying objects, and sun glare is the job of safety goggles.

Cycling jerseys often have foam or gel padding sewn into them, particularly at the elbows. Full-length pants come equipped with extra cushioning at the knees and in the seat. For those who are extra concerned about safety there is body armor. Some extreme bike riders wear gloves. Leather palms let them grip their bike's handlebars tighter and prevent scrapes and cuts in case of a fall.

Safety footwear does not really exist. However, shoes with thick rubber soles, or bottoms, can keep a rider's feet from slipping off the bike's pedals, and that definitely reduces accidents.

CHAPTER FOUR

READY TO RACE

When it comes to entering and winning extreme biking competitions, riders should think about climbing a ladder. Local races, which is how most people start, pit riders from one city and nearby towns against each other. Finalists and winners at the local level are then qualified to enter regional events. There they will be challenged by racers from cities and towns in the same geographic area. From there, the best extreme bikers move on to state or provincial races, which can lead all the way to the nationals. The very best in the world are sure to make an appearance at an international championship race or series of races. Then there are the events that are considered extra-special in sports circles. Extreme biking has been featured, in one form or another, at the Olympic Games and the X Games since the 1990s.

33

BMX racers navigate a jump during a semifinal heat at the 2012 Olympic Games in London.

None of this ladder climbing or bike riding would be possible without the groups that organize and sponsor competitive cycling events. More than just a chance to hand out trophies, these races are a chance to show extreme biking in its best light. Racers, wanna-be extreme cyclists, and spectators alike benefit from organized cycling events at all levels.

EXTREMELY UNITED STATES

No matter the style of biking, USA Cycling is "event central" within the United States. More than three thousand events get the organization's support and official seal of approval. Among the eighteen national titles awarded by USA Cycling each year are championship events in BMX, cross-country, downhill (called "gravity"), and marathon mountain biking. All skill and age levels are covered, and there is even a separate USA Cycling Collegiate Mountain Bike Championship.

The organization also looks to the future of cycling by providing guidance and training. The USA Cycling National Development Program essentially scouts for talented riders at the local and regional levels, offering spots at training camps and opportunities to otherwise work with professionals toward national and world cup titles.

RACING FOR THE CUP

National championship events are held by Cycling Canada in BMX and a handful of mountain biking styles, including downhill and cross-country. Yet extreme biking in Canada revolves mainly around cup series events in mountain biking and BMX. A cup series is made up of a group of races run over a period of time, usually months. Riders earn points for where they finish in the race. After the last race of the series is run, the rider with the most points wins.

The Cycling Canada Cup series for BMX started in 2012; it takes place in several cities in various Canadian provinces. In 2014, a total

SUPER EXTREME MOUNTAIN BIKING

Home to Mount Everest, the highest mountain peak in the world, the Himalayas also play host to one of the most exciting and rewarding mountain bike races in the world. The Trans Himalayan Challenge is a cross-country race that takes ten days to complete. More than 340 miles (550 km) are covered at elevations upward of nearly 33,000 feet (10,000 m). There are four divisions of racers: men's, women's, and master's (over forty), which are all solo rides, and teams of two bicyclists. To participate in the Trans Himalayan Challenge, riders must be at least eighteen years old and in terrific health.

A bicyclist races high up in the Himalayan Mountains. Events such as the Trans Himalayan Challenge are some of the most extreme mountain biking races on Earth.

of nine races were run before a winner took the title. The cup series for mountain biking is split between two styles, cross-country and downhill. There is a series of three or four races for each style.

Cycling Canada helps up-and-coming athletes who are at the Olympic or world cup level of extreme biking by providing coaching, help with college tuition (if needed), and a small amount of money for basic living expenses.

THE GLOBAL REACH OF EXTREME BIKING

At the international level, Union Cyclist International (UCI) is the governing body for cycling as a competitive sport. Headquartered in Switzerland, UCI establishes and enforces rules and regulations regarding equipment and races around the world. Several extreme biking title races are held each year courtesy of the organization. These include the Mountain Bike World Cup, the Mountain Bike Marathon World Championships, and the Mountain Bike and Trials World Championships. World championship BMX events are also on UCI's list of races, as is the Trials World Cup.

In addition to governance, UCI also offers training for riders in the hopes of leading them to world cup or even Olympic races and titles. In support of riders everywhere, the organization also offers training for coaches and cycling mechanics. Additionally, the UCI Bikes for the World program gives quality bicycles to riders who are associated with approved national biking groups but unable to get such equipment on their own.

BEFORE THE CARVE AND GRIND

Hopping on an off-road bike and carving (taking the curves of a twisty mountain road at high speeds) or grinding (a BMX trick where part of the bike grinds along an obstacle) right away is tempting. However, there are a few things anyone who wants to get into extreme biking should do before hitting the trail or track. Finding the right bike—for the rider's height, skill level, and style of extreme biking—is a very important first step. Not having the right bike is like trying to do a job properly but not having the right tools. The same goes for other riding gear.

Learning and adopting safety measures are also absolute musts for extreme bikers, especially beginners. Other mountain bikers and BMX racers can provide good information on what they do and wear during races—what seems to work for them based on actual, firsthand

A mountain biker—wearing pads, a helmet, and an activity monitor—carries his bike up a steep hill. Preparation for extreme biking includes equipment and fitness.

experience. Local cycling clubs on through to national organizations can provide all the details anyone could need about protective gear and smart ways to ride a bike so as to stay fast but safe.

Taking precautions is all part of being prepared for the "extremeness" of mountain biking and BMX. So, too, is getting and staying physically fit. It takes a lot of upper-body strength to maneuver a bike over rough ground, around tight turns, and through jumps and tricks. Likewise, a rider's leg and butt muscles need to be in great shape for pedaling and power. A strong core is also important because that is a large part of what gives riders good balance.

Finally, extreme bikers should have fun. They ought to get excited about the thrills that mountain biking and BMX offer, get pumped, and enjoy the ride.

GLOSSARY

berm A man-made banked corner on an extreme biking course.

endurance The ability to do something for a great length of time.

enduro A race held in stages across long distances and multiple trails of rough ground, usually on bicycles, motorcycles, or motor vehicles.

governance The ability of an individual or group to control how an organization acts or proceeds.

incline An upward slope.

jersey A shirt made of special fabric and designed especially for athletes.

klunker A classic bicycle that is fitted with special equipment to make it better able to take a beating—and perform better—as a mountain bike.

leathers A pair of bike-riding pants that are meant to be like protective clothing worn by motorcylists.

modified Having certain parts changed so that something is improved or acts differently than it originally did.

motocross A type of motorcycle racing that takes place on a dirt track with jumps, hills, and tight turns.

obstacle Something that makes action and movement difficult.

promoter A person who organizes and gives support to an event or performance.

repurposed Changed so that something is usable in a new way.

resistance A force moving against something; bicycle racers try to reduce wind resistance so they can move faster.

steep Almost straight up and down.

terrain An area of land or ground.

FOR MORE INFORMATION

The American Bicycle Association
1465 W. Sunrise Boulevard
Gilbert, AZ 85233
(480) 961-1903
Website: http://usabmx.com
Operating under the name USA BMX, the American Bicycle
   Association is considered the lead BMX governing association in
   North America. The main thrust of the organization is to organize
   BMX races throughout the United States, Canada, and Puerto Rico.

Cycling Canada
21 / Riverside Drive, Suite 203
Ottawa, ON K1H 7X3
Canada
(613) 248-1353
Website: http://www.cyclingcanada.ca
Cycling Canada's mission is to promote the sport of cycling and
   develop athletes that are among the best in the sport. Among the
   organization's programs are CAN-BIKE, a series of courses on
   bike riding and safety, and Race Clean, which stresses fair play
   and personal achievement.

International Mountain Bike Association Canada
P.O. Box 23034
Kitchener, ON N2B 3V1
Canada
(855) 255-4095
Website: http://www.imbacanada.com
Founded in 2004, IMBA Canada is the Canadian national arm of the
   International Mountain Bike Association. IMBA Canada is a nonprofit

organization that builds and maintains mountain biking trails, advocates for the sport with political organizations, and gathers riders together to feed passion for the sport.

Marin Museum of Bicycling and Mountain Bike Hall of Fame
1966 Sir Francis Drake Boulevard
Fairfax, CA 94930
(415) 450-8000
Website: http://mmbhof.org
Dedicated to preserving the history of the sport, the Mountain Bike Hall of Fame became a part of the Marin (CA) Museum of Bicycling in 2014. Press clippings, memorabilia, race photos and video, and even a few vintage bikes are part of the hall's collection.

National Off-Road Biking Association (NORBA)
c/o USA Cycling
210 USA Cycling Point, Suite 100
Colorado Springs, CO 80919
(719) 434-4200
Website: http://www.usacycling.org/norba.htm
A division of USA Cycling, NORBA sanctions mountain bike races across the United States, including two juniors series. Among the organization's other programs are mountain biking camps, equipment clinics, and access to coaches.

United States Extreme Sports Association
6350 Lake Oconee Parkway
Suite 102-128
Greensboro, GA 30642
(877) 900-8737

Website: http://usesa.org
The United States Extreme Sports Association is an umbrella
organization that oversees discounts on equipment and services
and an extreme-sports social network.

WEBSITES

Because of the changing nature of Internet links, Rosen Publishing has
developed an online list of websites related to the subject of this book.
This site is updated regularly. Please use this link to access the list:

http://www.rosenlinks.com/STTE/Bike

FOR FURTHER READING

Anderson, A. J. *Adrenaline Rush: BMX Biking*. Mankato, MN: Smart Apple Media, 2012.

Benjamin, Daniel. *Sports on the Edge: Extreme Mountain Biking*. Salt Lake City, UT: Benchmark Books, 2011.

Hamilton, S. L. *X-Treme Sports: Biking*. Edina, MN: ABDO Publishing, 2010.

Labrecque, Ellen C. *BMX Racers*. Berkeley Heights, NJ: Enslow Publishers, 2010.

Mason, Paul. *Mountain Biking*. New York, NY: Rosen Publishing, 2011.

Polydoros, Lori. *BMX Greats*. Mankato, MN: Capstone Press, 2011.

BIBLIOGRAPHY

Bainbridge, Eric Gordon. "Repack Downhill." Mountain Bike Roots, January 23, 2009. Retrieved November 2014 (http://www.mountainbikeroots.com/events/repack.php).

BMXUltra.com. "Scot Breithaupt: The History of BMX." August 11, 2003. Retrieved November 2014 (http://bmxultra.com/interview/scotb).

Breeze, Joe. "Repack History." Marin Museum of Bicycling and Mountain Bike Hall of Fame. Retrieved November 2014 (http://mmbhof.org/mtn-bike-hall-of-fame/history/repack-history/).

British Cycling staff. "Get into Mountain Biking." British Cycling. Retrieved November 2014 (http://www.britishcycling.org.uk/mtb/article/20131213-Get-into-Mountain-Bike-0).

Carruth, Mike. "A Partial History of the Sport of BMX Racing." Vintage BMX, December 2011. Retrieved November 2014 (http://www.bmxnews.com/pdf/history_of_bmx_timeline_1211.pdf).

Coombs, Charles. BMX: A Guide to Bicycle Motocross. New York, NY: William Morrow and Co., 1983.

Encyclopedia Britannica. "History of the Bicycle." Encyclopaedia Britannica Online. Retrieved November 2014 (http://school.eb.com/levels/middle/article/273207).

Kelly, Charlie. "NORBA History." Charlie Kelly's website. Retrieved November 2014 (http://www.sonic.net/~ckelly/Seekay/norba.htm).

Kelly-Clyne, Luke. "Bike Trials Starter Guide." The Adrenalist, October 2012. Retrieved November 2014 (http://www.theadrenalist.com/sports/bike-trials-starter-guide/).

Marks, Ben. "The Hippy Daredevils Who Were Just Crazy Enough to Invent Mountain Biking." Collectors Weekly, September 9, 2014. Retrieved November 2014 (http://www.collectorsweekly.com/articles/the-hippie-daredevils-who-were-just-crazy-enough-to-invent-mountain-biking).

McCormick, David. "The Buffalo Soldiers Who Rode Bikes." HistoryNet. November 2012. Retrieved November 30, 2014 (http://www.historynet.com/the-buffalo-soldiers-who-rode-bikes.htm).

Nolte, Carl. "A Piece of Railway History Returns to Mt. Tam." *San Francisco Chronicle*, February 24, 2009. Retrieved November 2014 (http://www.sfgate.com/bayarea/article/A-piece-of-railroad-history-returns-to-Mt-Tam-3249930.php).

Ord, Chris. "Origins of Mountain Biking." *Outer Edge*, July 29, 2010. Retrieved November 2014 (https://www.youtube.com/watch?v=DLH8GWuejyo).

Outdoor Participation Foundation staff. "2014 Outdoor Participation Topline Report." Outdoor Industry Association. Retrieved November 2014 (http://www.outdoorfoundation.org/pdf/ResearchParticipation2014Topline.pdf).

Sandsbury, Scott. "Fat Tires Keep 'Freak Bikes' Rollin' Over All Sorts of Terrain." *Yakima Herald Republic*, November 6, 2011. Retrieved November 2014 (http://www.heraldnet.com/article/20111106/SPORTS/711069918).

Smithsonian Institution. "Breezer 1 Mountain Bike." The National Museum of American History. Retrieved November 2014 (http://americanhistory.si.edu/collections/search/object/nmah_1419571).

Swiger, Zachary. "Bike Trials 101 at Colorado Northwestern Community College." Bike Trials.com. April 18, 2005. Retrieved November 2014 (http://biketrials.com/articles/ColoradoNorthwestern/index.shtml).

Tunney, Brian. "Dew Tour Adds Flatland as BMX Discipline." X Games, August 15, 2012. Retrieved November 2014 (http://xgames.espn.go.com/bmx/article/8271775/dew-tour-returns-ocean-city-md-adds-flatland-discipline).

Union Cycliste Internationale. Retrieved November 2014. (http://www.uci.ch).

USA-BMX staff. "History." Retrieved November 2014 (http://usabmx.com/site/sections/7).

INDEX

ABOUT THE AUTHOR

Jeanne Nagle is an author and endurance athlete who respects and admires those who wheel their way into extreme biking. Among her other Rosen titles are *Careers in Coaching; Archie, Peyton, and Eli Manning* (Sports Families); *Sidney Crosby* (Living Legends of Sports); and *Kiteboarding and Snowkiting* (Sports to the Extreme).

PHOTO CREDITS

Cover, p. 4 (biker) © iStockphoto.com/mgkaya; cover, pp. 1, 3, 6, 15, 26, 33 (landscape) © iStockphoto.com/MorelSO; p. 5 Connor Walberg/Stone/Getty Images; p. 6 Print Collector/Hulton Archive/Getty Images; pp. 9, 16–17 © AP Images; pp. 12–13 Kirby/Hulton Archive/Getty Images; p. 18 Vocal Image Comm., LLC/Stockbyte/Getty Images; p. 22 Trevor Williams/Taxi Japan/Getty Images; p. 24 Digital Light Source/Universal Images Group/Getty Images; p. 28 Sinelyov/Shutterstock.com; p. 30 (top) Minerva Studio/Shutterstock.com; p. 30 (bottom) Purestock/Thinkstock; p. 31 Heath Korvola/Stone/Getty Images; p. 33 (inset) Mike Powell/Sports Illustrated/Getty Images; p. 35 © Doug Blane/Doug Blane Photography/Alamy; p. 37 Justin Lewis/Stone/Getty Images; cover and interior pages graphics SkillUp/Shutterstock.com, Sfio Cracho/Shutterstock.com, saicle/Shutterstock.com, Frank Rohde/Shutterstock.com, Thomas Bethge/Shutterstock.com, nortivision/Shutterstock.com, PinkPueblo/Shutterstock.com.

Designer: Michael Moy; Editor: Heather Moore Niver